Professional

Copyright 2012 Steven Starklight

Contents

Author's Preface:

Introduction:

Chapter 1: Getting Your Voice

Chapter 2: Attribution

Chapter 3: Cop Speak

Chapter 4: Distractions

Chapter 5: Improving Your Writing

Excerpt from *Police Daily Journal; Tongue in Cheek True Stories*:

Author's Preface:

I wrote this book about eight years ago. A lot has happened in eight years. A lot has changed in our profession. In fact, it's almost unrecognizable to the state of policing when I started in 1993. Luckily, a few things have not changed, and one of them is the need for cops to write properly. That will never change.

There are a lot of books out there that are geared to law enforcement officers (LEOs) and report writing. Most of them are a lot longer and more comprehensive than mine, and that's ok. My book won't be able to turn you into Mark Twain overnight- or ever.

I assume the majority of you already know the basics. The goal of my book is to show you some of the most common mistakes that I see LEOs make in their writing, and give you the tools you need to avoid making those mistakes, and to write a more bulletproof report.

Since 2012, I've had some time to think about this book, and whether it's sufficient. With COVID-19, I've had a lot more time to think, and to write. Therefore, it is with a great deal of excitement that I inform you that within the week, I will publish *Grammar Saves Lives, Volume 2*, with more lessons, more material. Look for it!

I wish you all the best in your pursuit of law, order, and justice.

Steven Starklight

August 2020

Introduction:

How many times have you found yourself sitting in a chair looking down at your incident report, dripping with red ink, wondering where you went wrong? Maybe you have sat in some lawyer's office on the receiving end of some verbal criticism about something you wrote, or failed to write, in a report. I specifically remember being in such a situation, listening to the assistant district attorney drone on, pontificating about all the ways my report would create problems at trial. I also remember imagining how that prosecutor would do in a uniform with a gun and badge dealing with the public and their problems.

There will always be someone willing to criticize everything you do. Just about everyone is an armchair critic of police procedure. It reminds me of a famous quote from Theodore Roosevelt, one that I had posted in my office when I was a police legal advisor to remind me where I stood in that agency. In fact, it embodies most of the reasons why I left the practice of law to return to law enforcement:

It is not the critic who counts: not the man who points out how the strong man stumbles or where the doer of deeds could have done better. The credit belongs to the man who is actually in the arena, whose face is marred by dust and sweat and blood, who strives valiantly, who errs and comes up short again and again, because there is no effort without error or shortcoming, but who knows the great enthusiasms, the great devotions, who spends himself for a worthy cause; who, at the best, knows, in the end, the triumph of high achievement, and who, at the worst, if he fails, at least he fails while daring greatly, so that his place shall never be with those cold and timid souls who knew neither victory nor defeat.

He is talking about you. He is talking about our police officers, our soldiers, those that devote their lives and their energy on "worthy causes." The role of the prosecutor (in criticizing your work), the role of police management, those in administrative roles, are all important, but it is the work you do on the street that makes the difference. Remember that.

You will see several quotes from President Roosevelt in this book, not because of some particular affinity he had for the police, or because he is my hero, but simply because he made some great statements that are quite relevant to our discussion.

Those of you with an astute eye are probably wondering why I would use a quote in a book on critical writing that minimizes the role of the critic and places the emphasis on one's deeds, not another's critique of those deeds. Well, first, it is a great quote!

Second, police officers fit perfectly in the role of the man in the arena. Prosecutors, supervisors, defense lawyers, citizens watching your every move, all these people will be critics of your work, all these cold, timid souls. The most important aspect of your job is in the field, but if you cannot properly document that work, then you will have problems. Your work in the arena will put a criminal behind bars; your written word is what will keep him there. That is why I use this quote. You must be a good LEO, but you must also be a good report writer. It really is that simple.

Police officers do not graduate from the academy and instantly know how to be critical thinkers and logical and technical writers. It takes a lot of practice. How often have you written a report and then, later, found yourself regretting something you wrote, or racking your brain trying to remember some relevant detail that you neglected to add? Are you frequently defending your writing as your supervisor or prosecutor picks it apart? Are you sick of it? You must be, because you bought this book, and I am going to make it worth every penny.

As a superior court judge once told me in the middle of a trial, "Counselor, the Devil is in the details!" He was right, so let's explore those details. Police officers are in a unique position in society. You must be fearless as a front line soldier, intelligent as a nuclear physicist, strong as an ox, and precise as a surgeon. You must not only have the requisite mental stamina and ability but the physical prowess to back it up. I defy you to identify a job with as much responsibility and as broad a set of conditions precedent as that of a beat cop.

And, as my lieutenant used to tell us at our squad meetings, nobody has more authority, more power, than a uniformed patrolman. To wield so much power, to have the brains and the brawn and the courage, to be able to balance all those characteristics makes for quite an individual. Unfortunately, it isn't enough. You must also be able to accurately document and describe your actions. That is where I come in. Your written work should be the mirror image, or reflection, of your work.

I cannot give you everything you need to be a successful police officer. That takes years and a lot of preparation and even a little luck. (If you are trying to break into the career, then I will insert a shameless plug for my other book, *How to Become a Police Officer: The Best Tactics to Get Police Officer Jobs and enter the Police Academy*.) This book is designed simply to address one aspect of what I believe is the most difficult (and rewarding) job in the country. The work police officers do is only as good as a police officer's ability to document it. Do not take this part of your job lightly.

This is not intended to be a back to basics guide to proper grammar, sentence construction and diagramming and all that high school stuff. There are plenty of much larger (and more expensive) books that cover those elementary rules and principles. This book presumes that you already know the difference between subject and verb, adjective and adverb. However, there are some basic rules and common mistakes with which you must be familiar when writing professionally, and I will make sure you understand them by the end of this book.

A word about the title: yes, it is catchy, and yes, the title was intended to draw people in and read my book. However, I firmly believe it is true. Grammar is one aspect of precision writing, along with punctuation, spelling, and content. Some of you are probably rolling your eyes, dismissing the priority I am placing on these topics. Let's look at a few examples. Here is an easy one: a man goes on a business trip for a few days. While he is away, he unwittingly sends the following text message to his wife:

Hi, having a great time in Vegas. Wish you were her.

I would guess the problem is fairly obvious. Proofread your work. When you finish proofreading it, put it down, walk away, then return and proofread it again. I just cannot emphasize that strongly enough.

If you do not pay attention to your writing, you could make as dangerous a mistake as our man on the business trip to Vegas.

Here's another great example, blatantly stolen from various blogs and websites on the Internet under the heading "Punctuation Saves Lives:"

Let's eat, Grandma!
Let's eat Grandma!

If the above requires explanation, your problems are way beyond my abilities. A comma is all that separates you from a happy day with family and life in prison!

By the way, take a closer look at this book: it is short and sweet. It is not a 300 page textbook with practical exercises and an examination at the end. It is not designed to be a college textbook. It is a down and dirty guide to professional writing for law enforcement officers. (By the way, for the rest of this book I will abbreviate law enforcement officer to LEO.) If you need special help on grammar, syntax, spelling and the like, get a book devoted to such things. I will give you some good ideas later in the book as to a few things that you should keep on your shelf when you are writing. As for you, my reader, this is a book written by a cop, for cops, about stuff that cops write about; nothing more, nothing less!

Now back to reality. Let's briefly discuss the necessity for precision in your writing. Compare, if you will, the following two excerpts taken from the same single (and imaginary) witness statement:

Frank told me that he told him Jones killed her, but not her friend. Frank said he last saw Jones at the corner of Fifth and Pine walking away from him holding a gun. Frank said that as he walked past that intersection he encountered Louise, and heard her tell him that Megan called him a jerk. Frank heard him tell her that he would kill her and that she was a bitch.

Frank said that Jones told Frank that Jones killed Jane, but not Megan. Frank said that he last saw Jones at the corner of Fifth and Pine walking south and holding a gun. Frank said that as Jones walked past that intersection he encountered Louise, and Frank heard Louise tell Jones that Megan called him a jerk. Frank heard

Jones tell Louise that he would kill Megan and that Megan was a bitch.

Reading the first statement, do you have a clue what Frank said? I certainly don't! Without precision and attribution (to be discussed shortly), your reports will have no value. In fact, they can actually provide *negative value*.

WAR STORY:

I was at an intersection in my car when someone threatened me with a gun. He was the passenger in a car that pulled up next to my car at the intersection. The passenger got out of his car, brandished a firearm, and threatened me. Just as I reached for my own weapon, another car pulled up between us in the empty third lane, and the attacker drove away. I called 911. A law enforcement officer (LEO) was dispatched to me to take my report and my statement. For whatever reason, this officer did not seem very interested in what I had to say. In fact, he was openly hostile.

The suspect was eventually arrested and the case went to trial. While meeting with the prosecutor, he provided me a copy of the LEO's initial incident report, which I had never read. I was shocked. I had provided the LEO exact quotes of the threat the suspect yelled, and an exact description of him, his vehicle, and even the weapon the suspect brandished. The LEO completely misquoted me, laid out the entire event incorrectly, and glossed over much of the detail I had provided. In short: he was a terrible writer.

On the day of trial, I spent two hours under cross examination. The defense attorney's weapon of choice was that LEO's initial report! Because of that officer's mistakes and indifference to the facts, not to mention his poor writing skills, we almost lost our case. His version of the facts was so warped that it made one of us look like a liar, and I promise you, I was telling the truth!

The war story I just told you is absolutely true, and one of several I will weave into the book if I think it is illustrative of a point I am trying to make. These are each true stories taken from my experience as a police officer or prosecutor or in one of my other law enforcement careers.

By the way, because I mentioned my experience, let me give you my quick resume. Perhaps you sought out this book after reading one of my others, like *Get a Gun and Badge Today* or *True Police Stories*. Then again, you might be reading this book because it was assigned to you at the police academy. Regardless of how you came across it, let me establish why I know what I am writing about: I have twenty years in the business, including time I spent as a prosecutor and as the legal advisor for a very large agency on the east coast. I started out as a uniform patrolman with a county police department, and have served over the years as a campus police officer, a district attorney's investigator, a deputy sheriff and for the last ten years as a special agent of the FBI. I have a degree in English, a Masters degree and a Juris Doctor (law degree). These were all studies that required a lot of professional, academic writing. I had to become a master of the *MLA*, the *Bluebook* and the *Elements of Style*.

I have been a prolific writer since I was a child, and still love to write, whether fiction or reference. I will tell you with no hesitation that what made my career so rewarding, so successful, has been my ability to write. I am good, but nothing special when it comes to shooting, to working cases, to physical agility or defensive tactics. However, I can write, and whether you believe it or not, writing is one skill that you cannot fake, and for which you cannot compensate in other ways. Just like your firearms instructors tell you about shooting, writing is a learned skill, and the concept of "muscle memory" applies with equal strength to writing. Just like you cannot have a friend take your test for you, cannot have your friend qualify with a handgun for you, you also cannot have another officer write your reports for you.

One last introductory concept I want to address: I called this book *Professional Report Writing for Law Enforcement Officers* because I am not addressing only police reports. I am also referring to evidence logs, witness statements, confessions (if you write them for the subject), anything in narrative form, whether it be for jailers, investigators, probation officers; the topics I will discuss in this book will, frankly, be of value no matter your career. In fact, even if you end up working in another field completely, much of what you will learn in this book will apply with equal importance.

Chapter 1: Getting Your Voice

Think back to college, or perhaps high school, when you learned about voice. We are going to focus on the two main voices used in our kind of writing: active and passive.

Compare the following:

I was told by the witness that a loud crash was heard, then a crowd of people were seen running past him.
The witness said he heard a loud crash, then a crowd of people went running past him.

Does the longer sentence give you more information? Does it somehow make the information more clear, or easier to digest? Does it sound more formal? Does it just sound better? I don't think so! In fact, the passive voice makes it a murkier, hazier story. Read the two examples again. *A crowd of people were seen running....* By whom? The witness? Someone else? In fact, is it clear that it was the witness who observed these events? Technically speaking, the witness could be saying that someone told him these facts. To put it simply: passive voice lacks precision and you should avoid it.

Now compare another set:

A witness statement was collected by me, then the report was written.
I collected the witness statement, then wrote the report.

In the first example, do you know with any degree of certainty who wrote the report? Is it clear whether it was the writer of the sentence? That report could have been written by anyone. Just like the first set of examples, does the lengthier statement somehow give us more information? No! In fact, the longer sentence adds nothing but ambiguity.

This is a good (albeit loose) example of a concept generally referred to as Occam's Razor. Occam's Razor stands for the principle that generally speaking, the simplest solution is usually the correct one. I see the issue of voice as one conducive to analysis with something close to Occam's Razor: I recommend that we apply what I have dubbed Occam's cousin Wilhelm's Razor: the simplest language is usually the best way to describe something. (Do not expect an academic to have ever heard of Wilhelm's Razor; I just made it up!)

Applying Wilhelm's Razor in the two examples I provided, the shorter and simpler sentences are the more clear, easier to comprehend ones. You cannot go wrong using the active voice. They are almost always shorter and more clear.

Just as Occam's Razor can generally be applied in almost every issue you encounter, our new friend Wilhelm's Razor will also be relevant in just about all writing. Let's restate Wilhelm's Razor one more time: the simplest language is usually the best way to describe something.

One more quick comment on Wilhelm's Razor: some of you may be intellectual giants; you may already have advanced degrees. Many of you may actually be smarter and better educated than your supervisor, or at least the person responsible for reviewing and approving your reports. With that as a backdrop, consider the following two examples:

The witness elucidated that the suspect appeared to be hoary headed and devoid of facial hair. The suspect brandished a dirk of golden hue, and demanded that I divest myself of my wallet.
The witness said the suspect had gray hair and was clean shaven. The suspect had a gold knife and demanded my wallet.

I promise you that there will be many readers of your report that will require a dictionary to figure out the first example. It serves no purpose to use a more complicated word when a more simple one if available. Describing a suspect as devoid of facial hair gives the reader no more information than describing him as being clean shaven. Unless there is a legitimate need, do not use complicated words.

Sometimes you must use complicated words:

I searched the car and found drugs under the seat.
I searched the car and found methamphetamine under the seat.

I think you get the picture.

In professional report writing, the goal is to make your writing simple, to the point, and devoid of mistakes, exaggeration or personal opinion (or at least limit the personal opinion). Some of the most famous writers in the world wrote entire literary works with nary a three syllable word. Think of Ernest Hemingway. His lean, direct writing style made him famous. When you are writing, think lean and direct. Use short words and short sentences.

So avoid passive voice. What else am I talking about when it comes to voice? A good report does not require many adjectives or adverbs, very few superlatives, and no slang (more on this topic in the chapter devoted to Cop Speak). Let's take a look at Wilhelm's Razor in action:

Driver 1 proceeded through the intersection and was involved in a traffic collision with Driver 2, who was also proceeding through the intersection. Both Driver 1 and Driver 2 stated that they perceived a green light indicating their right to proceed through the intersection. Driver 1 and Driver 2 collided in the intersection, both claiming they had the green light.

So tell me this: which statement gives you more information? The first one? Read them carefully, and you will see they both give you the same details. The difference is that the second statement gives you the same information in 16 words that the first statement took 44 words to describe.

Let's review one more selection, this time an excerpt from a DUI arrest.

The drunk stumbled out of his car and blabbered something that sounded really stupid, then fell over on the ground. He was cuffed and stuffed by me.
The driver stumbled out his car, muttered something unintelligible, then fell over on the ground. I handcuffed him and secured him in the back of my patrol car.

The first example violates just about all the rules. The writer documented his personal opinion ("the drunk," "sounded really stupid"), used slang ("cuffed and stuffed"), and the passive voice ("cuffed and stuffed by me"). The personal opinion here serves no real purpose but to editorialize and suggest that you, as a witness, may even have a personal bias against drunk drivers. Nobody likes drunk drivers, but calling him a drunk and calling his behavior stupid does not further the criminal case and will guarantee an extra twenty minutes for you under cross examination.

QUICK TIP:

Many departments still handwrite the majority of their reports. Some departments have on-board computer systems into which you can type your reports. Some states still require specific forms for traffic collisions that must be printed in hand writing. Either way, professional writing will be important. A unique problem in using a computer is relying too much on spell check, grammar check and similar tools. In many cases, these programs are just plain wrong. If you don't understand the rules that these programs apply, then you will not know when to ignore the computer and when to correct the mistakes it finds. This is especially true when dealing with words that are spelled differently based on context:

The book is over there.
It is their book.
They're coming to get the book.
Spell check will probably not be able to distinguish between these spellings.

This book is designed to do more than prepare you to write police reports; it is designed to prepare you to properly complete any and all professional writing. You should be able to apply what you are learning here to even an evidence slip that requires nothing more than a signature. With that said, no matter what you are writing, and no matter the medium or the purpose, you should avoid having your handwriting look like the prescription your doctor hands you. You know the prescriptions I am talking about; the ones that always leave you with a look of amazement when the pharmacist glances at it and actually understands it. When completing a form, writing a narrative, even merely signing a document, there should be no question as to its content. Clarity is King.

In sum, use active voice whenever possible, avoid jargon, slang and avoid documenting your personal opinions unless they are conclusory and have value. For example: *I determined that the driver was less safe.* Or perhaps: *I placed him under arrest because I believed he remained a threat to his family.* To write *I arrested the stupid drunk* would be an improper documentation of your personal opinion.

Another concern in professional report writing is tense. You should avoid using present tense in your report writing. It is grammatically incorrect and awkward:

The witness says that he saw the suspect smashing the window.
I order the suspect out of the car

As a general rule, you should write in the past tense:

The witness said that he saw the suspect smash the window.
I ordered the suspect out of the car.

When relaying the facts to you, witnesses will often speak in present tense. When describing traumatic events, sometimes a witness will drift into present tense as they relive those traumatic events. To the extent you are recording verbatim quotes, the use of present tense may be appropriate. Witnesses giving you a statement in present tense is unavoidable. However, when you are the speaker, or the actor about whom you are writing, the use of past tense is more correct:

I ordered the suspect out of the car.
After checking the intersection, I drove down Mulberry Street.

By the time you are writing your report, the action you are describing, the statements you are recording, have already occurred. Past tense should be the tense of choice in all professional report writing.

In close, your report writing should generally be in active voice and past tense.

Chapter 2: Attribution

Let's briefly revisit our example from Chapter 1 and our friends Frank and Jones.

Frank told me that he told him Jones killed her, but not her friend. Frank said he last saw Jones at the corner of Fifth and Pine walking away from him holding a gun. Frank said that as he walked past that intersection he encountered Louise, and heard her tell him that Megan called him a jerk. Frank heard him tell her that he would kill her and that she was a bitch.

Frank said that Jones told Frank that Jones killed Jane, but not Megan. Frank said that he last saw Jones at the corner of Fifth and Pine walking south holding a gun. Frank said that as Jones walked past that intersection he encountered Louise, and Frank heard Louise tell Jones that Megan called him a jerk. Frank heard Jones tell Louise that he would kill Megan and that Megan was a bitch.

One of the main problems here is that of attribution. Attribution is the proper identification of the speaker of a statement, the doer of a deed, even a quality of a thing. In professional report writing for law enforcement officers, pronouns are the antithesis of attribution. *She, He, Him, Her, They, Their*, are all pronouns that can make a professional report confusing or even downright unintelligible.

How many times has someone said to you: "you know, they say that if you suck on a penny it will mess up the reading on a breath test" or "hey, they say that locking your doors improves the structural integrity of your car by 20%." I had a law school professor who would call on students by surprise during class. An unprepared student sometimes answered by saying "they say...." We have all begun a sentence with "they say...." Well, this professor would not accept such an answer. His response was usually something like this:

"They? They? Who is they? Why do I care what 'they' have to say?"

In short: pronouns are bad. References to pronouns might work for social conversations, but not professional report writing.

Let us now dig a little deeper.

There is another issue here, one that straddles both the topics of attribution and voice: it comes most often in affidavits. When writing about one's own action, LEOs tend to refer to themselves in third person:

Officer Starklight then detained him.
Your Affiant then detained him.

If I am writing this report, then it would be more clear, and easier to read, to say:

I then detained the driver.

Or, even better:

I detained the driver.

The interesting thing to note here is that the better sentence is both more specific and more general. If I am writing the report, and my name is at the bottom of that report, then there is really no reason to refer to myself by name.

Officer Starklight then detained him.

On the other hand, to whom does *him* refer? In context, it would likely be the driver. However, why leave such things to chance? If you are the speaker, refer to yourself as *I*. However, the object of your action in the sentence, *him*, should be more specific: *the driver*.

Also of note: the word *then* does nothing for the sentence. We like to fill blank space with words. Humans cannot stand silence. The next time you are interviewing a suspect, ask him or her a question and just wait. Don't say a word. The majority of people will not be able to handle the silence and try to fill it. Once you are aware of this concept, you will be amazed how often your fellow LEOs also cannot help themselves. Adding *"I guess"* to an answer, or *"Well, . . ."* or ending a sentence with *"you know what I mean?"* These are all gap fillers that have no useful purpose.

The same thing obtains on the written page: when writing professionally and with precision, you should scrutinize every single word and if it is neither required nor useful, you should get rid of it.

I then decided that, well, I might as well arrest him and place him in custody.
I decided to arrest him.

Does the first sentence give the reader anything more than the second? In fact, is even the second sentence as precise as it could be?

I arrested him.

Isn't that even cleaner?

Attribution is relevant for affidavits, for incident reports, and is most important when documenting witness statements, confessions and the like. When documenting the statements of others, always make sure it is perfectly clear to the reader who said what.

One theme that you can apply in your writing (and when providing testimony) is to imagine the way you would speak in social, semi-formal settings. I say semi-formal because when you are at a picnic with your friends, your language would likely be filled with slang and improper grammar, not to mention a lot of "you know what I mean" and "they say…." However, if you are at the office Christmas party and speaking with the police chief, you would most likely try to speak with proper grammar, avoid slang, and maintain subject-verb agreement. That is how your reports should read and how your testimony should sound.

This is a fairly straightforward topic, so let's look at a few examples of proper and improper attribution. These examples should be illustrative of the problems that can accrue:

I pulled him over and he yelled "it wasn't me!"
I pulled the driver over and the passenger yelled "it wasn't me!"

I chased him into the tree-line after he yelled "screw you, pig!"
I chased the male into the tree-line after his wife yelled "screw you, pig!"

A unique problem with attribution is that by failing to provide it in everything you write, you risk yourself forgetting who made the statements you recorded. I have written affidavits that do not become relevant in a case until years later. In re-reading my own words, I sometimes have difficulty recalling the speaker of some of the statements I recorded. If not for the prosecutor, then do it for yourself! You will write (and probably already are writing) reports every day. Day after day, month after month, into years, sometimes cases take a very long time to proceed through the judicial system. Do you think that once the criminal case is over that you are done? Guess again!

WAR STORY

I worked a traffic collision, citing both drivers because, in my estimation, both were at fault. At trial, the judge decided to dismiss both citations and let the insurance companies fight it out. I figured that was the end of it. In fact, years later, after I left the department to go to law school, I received a telephone call from a civil lawyer. Naturally, the insurance companies were unable to settle the claims, and the case ended up in litigation. Several years later, long after the criminal case was dismissed, this civil case was preparing for trial. I was subpoenaed to provide deposition testimony. I had no real recollection about anything, and barely remembered taking the accident report that was provided to me during the deposition. In short; my deposition was probably not very helpful to anyone. It brings to mind the classic (and comical) joke about the standard DUI reports submitted by old school state patrol officers throughout the nation: *"Saw drunk. Arrested same."*

In my example here, it would have been a good idea for me to have taken a more complete report, quoting witnesses, quoting the drivers, describing with better detail the scene upon my arrival, but instead, I took a fairly bland, non-descriptive report. The case suffered for it, and I was somewhat embarrassed years later sitting in my videotaped deposition. During those days when I was a police officer, we were short handed, and I recall being dispatched from one collision to another, going from call to call with no break. We did not have the time to take detailed reports, and that is an issue with which many departments and many officers must cope. Ideally, at the end of the shift, an officer will spend the extra time to make all his or her reports as accurate and detailed as possible so they will remember what happened months, or possibly even years later. As a practical matter, that is not always possible. For that reason, my suggestion is this: take as much time as you possibly can to produce a detailed, correct report. Go the extra mile in making sure it is accurate and complete. It will pay you dividends in the long run.

Chapter 3: Cop Speak

Every LEO has spoken in cop speak at some point in their career. After the end of shift, at the local bar, how many of you have shared a story about a 10-80, or about a "44 in progress?" You cannot help it! This is cop speak. Good radio discipline requires the use of signals and codes, but when documenting your actions in a report, you should avoid cop speak. That means refraining from the use of signals, codes, and police lingo. Some of that lingo is obvious and should be avoided: *perp, code 4, low sick.*

Sometimes cop speak is not only acceptable, but necessary to properly describe your behavior:

I Mirandized the suspect.
I read the driver the Implied Consent Warning.

The key is to know the difference between necessary lingo/cop speak and unnecessary. One good rule of thumb: if someone who is not a LEO can read your report and understand it, then it might be ok. Think of one of your parents reading your report. Mom and Dad will probably understand that you Mirandized someone, but will probably not know the difference between a Signal 2 and a Signal 3 (where I come from, it is the difference between an audible and silent alarm).

Certain phrases like the two I used above (*Miranda, Implied Consent*) are necessary. They are not slang or a contraction (*perp = perpetrator*). They are technical terms, or words of art. There is no other way to refer to them without greatly lengthening your report, and they have become a part of common understanding in the community. By the way, that concept of being woven into the fabric of society is so important that the United States Supreme Court cited it as one of the reasons why Miranda could not be overruled!

So in short, certain examples of cop speak are so ingrained that their usage has become popular enough to make them acceptable, and as we learned with Wilhelm's Razor, these phrases are much more concise than having to describe the concept. Imagine the following:

I read the suspect his rights as guaranteed to him under the Fourth Amendment of the United States Constitution and memorialized in the United States Supreme Court case of Miranda v. Arizona. *I informed him of his right to remain silent, his right to have counsel appointed....*

Isn't it easier to just say:

I Mirandized the suspect.

I think you get the idea.

Another trap LEOs fall into is stilted, stuffy, formal language. This is a particularly insidious subset of cop speak, because they are all normal, non-law-enforcement type words that have been adopted by the law enforcement community. Let's look at an example:

I proceeded through the parking lot, where dispatch had advised the complainant was waiting.

This might be a touchy section. Some of you have probably incorporated much of the contents of this chapter into your daily report writing, and will be clutching these old favorites to your chest as I ask you to give them up. Take a deep breath, then say your last "advised" or "proceeded" and let them go. In the immortal (and sometimes disputed) words of William Faulkner, you must "kill your darlings." In other words, those words to which people clutch so dearly are almost always the ones that need to be eliminated. Faulkner was referring to characters in books of fiction, but the premise is the same.

Back to our example:

I proceeded through the parking lot, where dispatch had advised the complainant was waiting.

This sentence has two main problems. It is written in passive voice, which is fertile ground for cop speak. Let's take this one apart.

Number one on the chopping block is *advised*. You are a LEO, not a lawyer. You aren't really in the advising business. When you tell someone something, you are doing exactly that. Your job is to make decisions and give direction. Rarely is it your job to provide advice. Generally speaking, perhaps 90% of the time, when you write in a report that you advised someone of something, you really just *told* them something. Don't glamorize it by calling it advice.

Furthermore, it is the very rare occasion when someone on a dispatch advises you of anything. The victim did not advise you of his injuries; he *told* you about his injuries. People tell each other many things, and on your dispatches or law enforcement activities, few will be truly *advising* you.

Proceeded is number two on my naughty list. The driver didn't proceed through the intersection; he drove through it. The jaywalker didn't proceed across the street; he walked! It is not incorrect in usage, but it is stilted and too general. People walk, people drive, people fly. People rarely proceed, at least not in ordinary usage. When was the last time you told someone that you proceeded somewhere? If someone walked, write that they walked; if they ran, write that they ran; if they drove through the intersection, then that is what you should write!

Also, eliminate the use of proceeded as a preparatory verb:

I proceeded to drive through the intersection.

This reminds me of my friends in the south, who are always "fixing" to do something.

I'm fixing to go out to eat.
I am proceeding to go out to eat.

Do these preparatory verbs really do anything to either sentence? Arguably, one could say *"I'm about to go out to eat."* That at least informs the reader that you intend to go out to eat shortly. *"I am preparing to go out to eat"* is better. *"I am proceeding to go out to eat"* sounds like you are doing it right now. It is imprecise and unnecessary.

Remember Wilhelm's Razor? Wilhelm's Razor would call for the elimination of "proceeding" in just about every sentence. It adds nothing but fluff and an air of stuffy formality. When someone asks you for directions, have you ever told them to proceed to the next street and turn left? Well, some of you probably have!

Stuffy: He fled on foot.
Better: He ran away.

Stuffy: They had an altercation.
Better: They had a verbal argument/physical fight.

Stuffy: He sustained a cut to his face.
Better: He was cut on his face.

Stuffy: I transported him to the hospital.
Better: I drove him to the hospital.

Stuffy: The victim was Code 4 at the scene.
Better: The victim was unharmed at the scene.

I think you get the picture, but before we move on, let me just mention one more word that you should eliminate from much of your professional writing: *Observed.* Mis-using this word makes a sentence too stuffy and vague.

I observed the victim had a cut to her face.
I observed the vehicle parked in the handicap parking spot.

Try these instead:

The victim had a cut to her face.
The vehicle was parked in the handicap parking lot.

Here are a few more:

I observed the vehicle drive by.

Try instead: *I saw/watched the vehicle drive by.*

I observed that he was shuffling his feet.

Try instead: *He was shuffling his feet.*

As you can see, Wilhelm's Razor would call for the elimination of *observed* in virtually all of these examples. *Observed* is only appropriate if it is important to describe that you personally witnessed something as it occurred:

I observed the driver back into the fire hydrant.

The word *observed* is similar to *proceeded* in that it is almost always mere filler; it does nothing but make a sentence bulkier. These words are the written equivalent of those little white Styrofoam peanuts that come in packaging materials. Leave them in the box and only pull out the valuables they were protecting! Only use them when they are absolutely necessary.

24

There is another subset of vocabulary commonly used by LEOs that need to be excised from professional report writing: words that aren't really words at all. The greatest offenders for LEOs are *"supposably"* and *"irregardless."* Perhaps I am old fashioned, but I refuse to accept these as real words. The legitimacy of the word *"Irregardless"* has been disputed for almost 100 years, and if a word has not made it into accepted usage in a century, there is no good reason to accept it now. As for *supposably*, it is, arguably, a word, but it has no place in the usages most commonly applied to it in professional writing. Do yourself, and the readers of your written word, a big favor, and get rid of these words. And while you are at it, toss *"exspecially"* in the can with them!

Slang and what I would call police vernacular also have no place in professional report writing. *Perp, bad guy, coms, vic.* These, and any iterations of them, should be avoided. *Perpetrator, suspect, subject, communications, victim*, these are neutral and acceptable. Perp is an improper shortening of perpetrator, and bad guy imparts a personal opinion that has no place in your report. You are not a made-for-television character like Officer Sipowitz from *Law and Order*. You are a professional LEO. Do not call suspects perps. Do you refer to other officers as *cops* in your reports? I have never seen it used. (By the way, do you know how police officers acquired the nickname *cop*? It is actually an abbreviation for *constable on patrol*.)

"I could care less." Ok, this is not an issue for professional writing, but it is a big one in speaking. If you can care less, that means in the grand scheme of not caring, there are many things that you dislike even more. 99% of the time, the speaker means to say "I could not care less," meaning that the thing to which the speaker refers is the very bottom on his list of things to care about.

Another confusion in terminology that I often hear, and one violated by a few lawyers I know: *moot* and *mute*. These two words have virtually nothing in common. It is almost never *a mute point*. A person that cannot speak is never *moot*. Let me give you just one example of correct usage for these two words.

It is a moot point because she already fled the scene.
The witness, a deaf mute, provided a written statement.

I have just a few more that I have heard in my time that I will address here. We are straying somewhat from the point of this chapter, but it will benefit you to read this section, and hopefully you will get a little laugh out of it.

Kick him to the curve. A famous comment made by motor officers nationwide. It generally means to perform a traffic stop. Unfortunately, it makes no sense. I can only assume the correct phrase is "kick him to the curb." If you must use such a phrase, at least say it correctly.

He was lit like a roman candle. Or, *he was a drunk.*

This could be a chapter in itself. When documenting someone's intoxication, use descriptive words, not conclusions or slang. In the incident report documenting a DUI arrest, your evidence that a driver was intoxicated is his slurred speech, his nystagmus at maximum deviation, his failure to successfully complete whichever field sobriety tests you administered. You should not document that he is *drunk, lit, toasted, shit faced, hammered* or anything similar. Just find and record the facts, your observations, and don't editorialize. Let the prosecutor make conclusions and charging decisions based on your evidence. Here is a thought: if the word you want to use to describe an intoxicated suspect is one that you have used when referring to yourself while out at a bar, it is probably not appropriate.

By the way, please indulge me with a slight diversion here. When an incident you investigated goes to trial, you will give the prosecutor a copy of your report. The prosecutor, through discovery, will hand a copy over to the defense. You will be questioned about your report and cross-examined about your report. So many of you might ask, what is the role of the incident report in a trial? Generally speaking, it is not evidence. It is not admissible as evidence in a criminal trial because it is hearsay. However, it *can* be used as the source of cross examination. It *can* be used by you as a testifying witness to refresh your recollection. It *will not* be admitted into evidence. The Rules of Evidence are beyond the scope of this book, and those rules are somewhat different in every state, so citing the rule of one state will not help those of you in any other state. For our discussion, just know that your report is not evidence but can (and will) be used against you!

QUICK TIP

I briefly touched on this earlier, but let me reiterate this point. Don't use cop speak in court. Jurors are more likely to connect with you, the arresting or citing officer, than they are with the lawyers. One of the main reasons jurors want to be on your side is that the jury considers the prosecutors and defense attorneys as part of the whole judicial system, along with the judge, the bailiff, and the other various personnel staffing a courtroom. Most of what comes out of the lawyers' and judge's mouths are unintelligible to the jury, a confusing and somewhat theatrical play acted out in a courtroom. They are the furniture in the courtroom. Their focus is on you.

The whole point of jury instructions prior to deliberation is to "dumb down" and explain the law the jury must apply when reaching their verdict. It is somewhat insulting as a juror to find that they are not trusted to simply read and apply the relevant statutes. You, as the star witness for the government, should not provide testimony that requires the jury to refer to a dictionary. To connect with them, your testimony must be simple, detailed and straightforward. After all, rare is the juror who "proceeds" to court to sit in the jury box. They *want* to like you and connect with you. Make it easy for them!

One more little diversion into the realm of courtroom testimony. Remember that law professor I mentioned earlier? He had another pet peeve with his students: the use of "I guess."

When a student started his response to a question of his and started with "I guess," it normally solicited a response from this professor close to the following:

"You guess? You guess? Are you paying all that money to go to law school to sit here and guess? If I want people to sit in my classroom and guess, I will just go pull a few of those landscapers outside into my class, sit them down right here in the front row and let them guess all day long. Are you a lawyer or a landscaper?"

And that student would never say "I guess" ever again.

Here is a free rule about courtroom testimony: never say you guess. Your guess is not admissible as evidence anyway, and it will anger many law school professors! Guessing is tantamount to speculation, and speculation is inadmissible in court.

Chapter 4: Distractions

This chapter is, in a sense, an expansion of everything else about which I have already written. All the issues we have discussed can each create distractions for your readers. Something we have not yet addressed that can be very distracting are simple mistakes. Typographical errors, misspellings, improper spacing, these can all distract the reader from the thrust of your writing. As a uniform patrolman, my reports had to be turned in before the end of my shift. Detectives have more time to complete their reports: they can document their investigation, set it aside, and review it the next day, with a fresh eye. Once you complete a report, ideally, you should set it aside and review it one more time for accuracy after letting some time pass. If you do not have this luxury, then you will have to review it for errors as soon as you finish writing it. You must teach yourself this discipline.

Back when I was writing incident reports, I wrote them in long hand and had to press down because we used three copy reports. If I misspelled a word or made a mistake my choices were to scribble out and try again, use liquid paper, or crumble it up and start over. If I chose liquid paper, I had to use three bottles, each a different color. White for the original, blue for the detective copy, pink for the third copy, the purpose for which I cannot remember.

In any event, it was understandable when an officer just scribbled out a word. These days, given the use of computers, mistakes are less tolerable.

As a general rule, your written work product should be perfect in every way. You should make that your goal. Limit the time you spend wishing you had added some fact, or left out something irrelevant. Limit the time spent listening to a defense attorney cross examining you about some imprecise statement you had placed in your incident report.

Avoid abbreviations. Your sergeant might understand them and approve your report for filing, but not the prosecutor, the defense attorney, the court, or the jurors.

I transported him to ADC.
I obtained a 10-17 for the suspect.
The arrestee kicked my MDT.

Try instead:

I drove him to the adult detention center (or jail).
I obtained a warrant for the suspect.
The arrestee kicked my mobile data terminal (or computer).

QUICK TIP

Here is another good reason to proofread your work: did you know that your reports may be subject to your state's open records act or sunshine act? The federal government has the Freedom of Information Act, which allows anyone to get a copy of a public record merely by asking for it. Just because a case you made has been resolved does not mean that your reports will not remain available for many years thereafter. A good defense attorney, in an effort to defend his client and make you look like a sloppy LEO, may file an open records request and review copies of every other arrest report you have ever made. If you are a sloppy writer, that could become a real problem. Do not place yourself in the position of having to defend your writing in court.

Here is another good reason: if you were to be sued for something you did as a LEO, the plaintiff's lawyer will demand, subpoena or request everything you have ever written. If your written work product contains careless errors, that lawyer will portray you as a sloppy officer that cuts corners and does not pay attention. Is that the reputation you want to have spread about regarding your work ethic? Minimize the criticism someone can lodge against you. Proofread your writing. Even Shakespeare has something relevant to contribute here:

"The evil that men do lives after them, The good is oft interred with their bones." (*Julius Caesar,* Act 3, Scene 2.)

A few days after you do something on the job, the only evidence left of your actions will be your written word. You could do all the right things on a dispatch, but if you do not properly record those things with your report writing, the only thing people will remember, or be exposed to in reviewing your work, is your documentation of your good deeds.

So, exactly which facts do you put in the report? Everything that is relevant. It is like the famous question asked of a famous sculptor: How do you take a block of marble and turn it into a gladiator on a chariot? The sculptor's answer: It is simple; I take my chisel and remove all the rock that does not belong and what is left is the gladiator on the chariot.

Leave out irrelevant details. Tell the whole story. Try to avoid making personal conclusions or giving personal opinions. One caveat regarding irrelevant details: I tend to document as much as I can because I want to be able to recall the incident. A year or two down the road when a certain case finally goes to trial, I will have to refresh my recollection of that incident, what people said, what I did, what exactly happened. Better to take an accurate, lengthy report and preserve your ability to recall the facts, than to have a bare bones report that gives the basics but not enough detail to give you the power of recall.

Take copious notes. Try to keep them. If your department has a method (or requirement) for storing them, use it. As a police officer I had a duffle bag filled with my old note pads. I had one in my back pocket my entire time on patrol, and everything I did went into those pads. Even after the passage of twenty years, I can open up one of those pads and instantly recall much of the dispatches during which I took those notes.

Those notes will make the difference from a barely acceptable incident report and one that tells the whole story and gives you the recollection you need to testify. The more you write, the better off you (and your reports) will be.

Use contractions sparingly, if at all. They generally have no place in professional report writing. Don't, can't, won't, shouldn't, these are not incorrect and not slang, but are informal and therefore inappropriate. You will find an occasional contraction in this book. However, this book is not an official report. It was designed to be informal to make it more readable. In professional report writing, however, contractions should be avoided. Imagine contractions in other professional documents.

This contract is legally binding; the parties can't derogate from the terms.
If the defendant doesn't report to probation, a warrant will be issued.

Do those quotes sound like they came from a binding contract or court order? How about these:

This contract is legally binding; the parties shall not derogate from the terms.
If the defendant does not (or fails to) report to probation, a warrant will be issued.

At the other end of the spectrum from contractions are long quotes. Avoid them. If you put something in quotation marks, you are indicating that what you wrote is exactly what the speaker said. Perhaps if you have a recording of the speaker, you will be in a better position to accurately quote the material. If the speaker says something particularly important, by all means quote it. The issue here is whether you should ever quote entire statements.

Let me make a suggestion: if you have the speaker on tape, then why not quote only the most important, most relevant parts, and forget the rest? If the person's entire statement is that important, then have someone else (or do it yourself) just transcribe the entire interview.

Here is another alternative: just burn the recording onto a CD and maintain it somewhere until the case is over. Again, you must refer to your agency's policies as to what you can do. My main point here is that if you must quote someone, make sure it is accurate. It is difficult to accurately quote someone, and that is why I suggest you avoid it. An example will better illustrate this point.

When I was a patrolman, upon the arrest of a driver suspected of DUI, we were required by state law to read what was called the Implied Consent Warning. We all carried little cards around, and read straight from them, our little belt mounted recorders busily recording our words and the driver's answer. Those cards seemed to change every few months, in direct response to court cases in which the language was successfully challenged. The cards changed color, and the dates were printed prominently upon them. Some officers wrote out the exact language of the card from which they were reading. I never did this, as it seemed unnecessary, and even worse, one single error in that language and you would find yourself in a long and painful cross examination trying to explain whether you read exactly from the card or whether you said exactly what you wrote in your incident report. Many of us kept all the old cards in a safe place in case a DUI arrest went to trial. I thought it was much better an idea to refer to the color and date of the card from which you read, and keep a copy of that card in case you did go to trial.

What is my point in the above paragraph? Do not directly quote something or someone unless you are not only certain of the quote, but confident that the quote itself is crucial to the successful resolution of your case.

Chapter 5: Improving Your Writing

Over time, practicing your professional writing will itself improve your professional writing. This may be somewhat of a syllogism, but it bears noting here. Writing improves over time. However, what do you think is the number one way to improve your ability to write? Reading!

Try to read every day. Read whatever you want. Read for pleasure. You won't even realize your writing skills are improving with every word you read. Your vocabulary will improve. You will recognize awkward writing, misspellings, improper tense, subject verb agreement; these mistakes will be as obvious as if they were printed in a different color.

Be an active reader. The meaning of many unfamiliar words will be clear from the context in which they are used. Those that do not reveal their true meaning should be looked up in a dictionary. If you are using an e-reader, you may even be able to just click the word and link straight to its definition. Technology is slowly removing any excuses you may have for not *actively* reading more often.

Also, write as much as you can. E-mails probably count if you try to make them real prose and not glorified text messages. Keep a journal. Write a short story or a letter to an editor. Your writing will improve. Get a pen pal. If you intend to start (or finish) college, try to take courses that require a lot of reading and writing. Such work will pay off dividends. If you are currently a college student, enroll in the courses that require term papers or at least regular writing assignments. The feedback you receive will be well worth it. If your agency offers training in report writing, take it. I would tell you to send me some of your reports for a critique, but I would quickly be overwhelmed by the response and my mailbox isn't big enough!

Go to a bookstore (or online) and buy *The Elements of Style* by William Strunk, Jr. and E. B. White (most popularly: "Strunk and White"). It is a short, pithy list of linguistic right and wrong and a requirement for any educated person's bookshelf. It is no bigger than *Grammar Saves Lives* and almost as easy to read. Let me give you one theme from this absolute-must-have book: *Eliminate needless words.* Needless words unnecessarily lengthens your writing and distracts the reader.

There are a few great websites that discuss redundant language, and there is a lot of it in professional law enforcement writing. Here are a few, straight out of the Department of Redundancy Department:

ATM machine = automated teller machine machine.
Completely eliminated = is there only a little bit eliminated?
The victim was completely dead = can one be partially dead?

Check out http://grammar.about.com/od/words/a/redundancies.htm. The title of this web page is *200 Common Redundancies.* The author, Richard Nordquist, lists these examples and many others.

The Internet is your friend. Many has been the time that, having forgotten a specific rule, I have typed a question into a search window on the Internet and 90% of the time, the first hit is the answer to my question. For example: what is the difference between e.g. and i.e.? Let's consider this a test. Type the preceding sentence into Google and click on the first result. I bet it gives you the answer. (If you do not have the Internet, just wait until the next page.)

There are a few other common errors you must avoid and that are always confusing. Luckily, these errors are so common that all you need to do is type the words into Google and press enter. The ones I see the most are *their* and *there, we're* and *were,* and *it's* and *its,* and so on. Do not be afraid to look up these words. These days, most LEOs have a smartphone and can get the answers to these questions while sitting in a patrol car. In my day, we carried dictionaries in our pursuit cases. These days, all you need is an I-Phone!

Those are some good general ideas. Now let's talk about some specifics to keep in mind when writing your report.

Common Errors

I considered not including these issues in the hopes of streamlining this book. However, these errors are so common, so distracting, that I decided to include them here. Let's start with my earlier example , **e.g. and i.e.**

Exempli gratia (e.g.) is Latin for "for example."
Id est (i.e.) is Latin for "that is."

35

My favorite cars are old American muscle cars, e.g., Mustangs, Chevelles, Cougars.
This is my favorite car; i.e., the Mustang.

There and Their

There tells you where. *Their* is possessive.

The suspects are over there.
These are their burglary tools.

Since and Because

Since involves time. Because tells you why.

He said he had been drunk since last Thursday.
Because you asked me, I will tell you.

It's and Its

It's is a contraction.

Its shows possession.

It's going to be a long night.
The dog chased its tail.

Could of Would of Could have Would have

Could of/Would of are just plain wrong.

I could have seen him if I had my glasses.
She would have gone to the gym if she was feeling better.

Organization / Consistency

Pick an order. It doesn't matter how you choose to organize your report, as long as it is organized in some fashion and that you are consistent with it. A lot of this section is dependent on your agency's paperwork, reporting requirements and general practice. I will try to stick with concepts that will be applicable to any situation.

In a prior career, long before law enforcement, I received some training as a forms consultant. There is actually quite a bit of thought that goes into the creation of a form for a business. In my experience, there are many law enforcement agencies that seem to put no thought at all into their layout. For example, have you ever noticed forms that contain a blank space for one's age that is twice the size as the blank space for one's name or address?

My point is this: do not assume that your agency's forms will cover all the relevant information that should be in the report itself. If there are boxes to fill to document a suspect's height, weight, hair color, eye color, build, complexion, race, gender, that is all useful information. However, if you just stick with the form information, you are doing your case a disservice. Was the suspect angry? Did he speak a foreign language? Did he have (or sustain) visible injuries during the crime? These are data that may be crucial to solving your case, but if you do not go the extra mile and document these observations, your case will suffer.

Perhaps the best example for this concept is the standard DUI report. Many agencies have tried to cover all the bases with their forms. There is a box to check for almost every observation, including every field sobriety test (FST) you could think of, and the results. These are great cues for an officer trying to cover everything. However, nothing beats a good, descriptive narrative. Checking boxes does not tell the whole story. People cannot "read" little check marks. People want to read a story, not hunt for little check marks. And, by the way, just checking boxes leaves a lot of information off the page. For example: which FST did you request from the driver first? Then which one? What if something strange happens during one of the FSTs? Is there a place to document observations on each one? That may need to go in your narrative.

So let's return to organization. Chronological order makes sense. What happened first? Then what happened? Then what? That sounds simple enough, right? Well, the question is upon which chronology will you rely? Let's say you have been promoted to detective (congratulations!) and have just completed a multiple witness, multiple day investigation. You now have an idea of what happened. For our example, say someone's home was burglarized, and you interviewed ten people in ten days. Let's also say that the victim has had someone living with them for two months and suspects they were involved. How do you order your report?

One method of chronological organization is to start with your first interview, then your next, then your next. In other words, your chronological organization is based on the interviews you conducted. This makes sense because it documents your interviews in the order you conducted them, which makes it clear why you didn't know to ask certain questions of your earlier victims, and why your knowledge of the facts improves the further into your investigation you go. Someone else can read your reporting and watch your investigation unfold.

On the other hand, reporting your investigation chronologically in this fashion can really muddle things up; your first witness could be the one that saw something suspicious the day after the burglary and the next witness could be someone that knew the roommate twenty years earlier. A reader new to the material might get lost very quickly.

You could also take all your witness statements, then write the report chronologically as to what happened. So here, your first paragraph might discuss the roommate moving in and why, then move on toward the suspicious activity of that roommate in the days before the burglary, then the burglary, then the aftermath. This paints a clear picture and lets an unprepared reader jump right in. The criticism for this approach is that it is much more difficult to organize because you must sort through all your witness statements and break them down into the right spot in your report. This can cause problems because it is much more prone to mistakes and can easily become very choppy to read.

Avoid duplication. I have seen investigations at certain agencies in which the investigator continually adds to his original report, and incorporates the narratives of his interview reports into this original report. This can get very confusing, especially for readers not familiar with the investigation. Further, the investigator never has a complete report. It will always be a work in progress.

There are other possibilities, although frankly, one of the above is generally your best bet. There are also some hybrids that take from both types of chronological interviews, then borrow from some other angles. Some LEOs may provide an introductory paragraph that lays out the complaint and the conclusion, then all the supporting facts. Other LEOs stick to the program, putting all the interviews into his or her report and moving on. As I mentioned earlier, the important thing is that you are consistent, and that other people can read your material and know exactly what happened.

There is one more comment on organization that I would like to share with you. Consider documenting your interviews and your investigative activity separately. One interview goes on one report; one investigative act goes in another. For example, you interviewed ten witnesses, so that is ten interview reports. You may have dusted the victim's home for prints, so that is one report. Then, say, you generated some leads and showed the witnesses some six packs. That would go on another interview report. Once you are finished with your investigation, you could gather up all your reports, then sit down and draft a narrative that combines all the salient features of your investigation. As you can imagine, this document could become your prosecutive memorandum, your probable cause statement for your arrest warrant, or your affidavit for a search warrant. In this manner you can minimize your duplicative work and focus on documenting what you are doing one time, then consolidate all that work at the end of the case.

No matter how you choose (or are told) to organize your writing, your reports will benefit greatly from taking proper notes during interviews and during investigations. The more complete and detailed your notes are, the better your report will be. In the case of a long investigation, those notes will be crucial in reconstituting all the information you have gleaned.

Do not rehash your entire investigation with each subsequent report. Many LEOs believe they must constantly add to their investigation as if they were adding chapters to a single novel. The first report they write may be a page, and the second two pages, and by the end of the investigation their reports are over 100 pages each. Perhaps this is personal opinion, but I fail to see the benefit to this method. The argument in favor of this method is that each report can stand on its own, and that if all the other reports are lost or destroyed, the reader will know the entire story from the most recent report.

There are several criticisms for this method. Here are two: first, with each new iteration of your report, you will have a larger number of former versions. Those versions may have found their way into many hands; supervisors, judges, attorneys. How will one know if they are looking at the most recent version? Second, the longer someone has to read to catch up to the new material, the less inclined they will be to read it. If you have a report that is twenty pages long and add two sentences to document subsequent information, you now must print a twenty one page report. Seems like a waste, doesn't it?

My perspective is as follows: if someone is reading one of my reports, the probability is very high that they already know why they are reading the report and the underlying facts that led to me writing it. Imagine how much unnecessary writing (and subsequent reading) would be required if, when documenting witness interview number ten in your burglary case, you had to summarize the entire investigation. It is simply not necessary. Anyone that wants to catch up with your case can read the previous reporting in your case file.

What if a week after you complete your investigation, you uncover new evidence, or a new witness appears with new information? Most agencies have some kind of addendum form or additional narrative form. Use one. Do not try to add the information to a report you already turned in. As long as the report file number is marked on the page, you should not need to rehash your entire investigation. This is especially relevant if you had a very long investigation, and/or the additional information is either of minimal use or minimal length.

Structure

Another thing that can be not only distracting but make it difficult to read your written word is that of structure. Long, run on sentences can kill someone's interest in reading your material. If you have not yet noticed, the paragraphs I have written in this book are intentionally very short. It makes for an easier, more pleasant reading experience, and should be incorporated into all professional law enforcement writing. If a paragraph is more than four or five sentences, there is a problem. That paragraph must be simplified and shrunk. I am not saying to eliminate the actual material; merely to shorten your paragraphs.

As a general rule, a paragraph should only contain one idea or one situation. For every new idea or situation, there should be a new paragraph. In professional report writing, it is best to minimize the length of your paragraphs. If you have a single idea or situation to document and you are exceeding three of four sentences, scrutinize your paragraph closely; chances are, you can break it down into smaller chunks. The point is to make it more digestible for the reader.

If you have a lot of paragraphs, consider adding sub-headings. You will have a hard time engaging a reader faced with a sea of words with no guideposts. If you have a very long investigative report, such as in the case of a murder investigation, the final product may require a table of contents. Do not make a prosecutor have to thumb through dozens of pages looking for what they need. How do you think you would enjoy this book if I failed to use sub-headings and chapters?

Details

The details of your reports will be very important. So what should be included in those details? I will try not to address police procedure, but one of the biggest examples of the importance in attending to details is in the suspect description. Think of the sculptor chiseling the gladiator on the chariot: put in everything that belongs and nothing that doesn't.

When you are drafting an incident report in which you have a witness providing a description of the suspect, that description should be very precise. That means asking the right questions so you can get the information you need. Perhaps the witness only saw the suspect for a second or two. Perhaps it was dark and they only saw a shadow. Do not simply become a recording device, writing down what you are told and moving on. You must dig. Witnesses are just that; witnesses are lay persons generally not accustomed to paying the level of attention to their environment like a LEO does. You will need to pry, poke, prod and ask round-about questions to get to the heart of the memories.

Say, for example, your witness is an elderly person and she is trying to explain the time of day she witnessed a suspect crawling into her neighbor's window. The elderly person states only that it was daytime. How can you pinpoint a better time estimate? What questions could you ask? Try asking your witness what they were doing at the time. Ask what was on the television, or whether she was taking any medication that day, whether she was eating and if so, what was she eating? The answers to these questions are completely irrelevant to the crime you are investigating. However, they are clues to when the crime occurred, and these odd questions will trigger memories that she may not find relevant, but will be excellent guide posts for you to arrive at a proper time estimate. If *Murder, She Wrote* was at the point where the heroine discovers the killer, then you know it was in the last five minutes of the hour in which that show was televised (unless your witness used Tivo, in which case you will need to try something else).

My commentary here is dangerously close to police procedure, and I don't want to tell you how to do your job; only how to write about it. The reason I brought up the questions to ask witnesses is to emphasize that some of these seemingly innocuous questions and their answers may become very important later. Read the following excerpt from a report:

The witness said she saw the suspect knocking on her neighbor's door, wait for a few minutes, then disappear. At that time, the witness was watching the beginning of Murder, She Wrote. *Later, as the show was ending, she saw the suspect walking around from her neighbor's back yard and climb into the back seat of a blue truck. The witness said she does not own a VCR or any other device that records television shows. The witness has Charter Cable.*

Ninety percent of the excerpt above has nothing to do with actual suspect information. However, it provides the prosecutor with some valuable information that will support and enhance the testimony of this witness when and if the case goes to trial. It provides enough information for one to establish fairly accurately when the suspect arrived and left, and almost exactly how long he was there. It also explains why the witness was able to recall the time that she saw the suspect. Should this information be in your report? Of course!

Something else that is important to keep in mind when documenting your interactions with witnesses: witnesses have five senses, and they all can provide useful information and all of their relevant sensory observations should be recorded. Observations can be equally and sometimes even more important than language.

Language can be subject to hearsay exceptions or a privilege, but observations are non-testimonial and almost always admissible as long as they are relevant. *Always document observations.* In the example of a DUI arrest, describe the driver's *appearance*: disheveled, red eyes, slurred speech, stumbling. Describe his *odor*: he reeked of alcoholic beverage. If your agency permits you to record witness statements, even better. Keep in mind, however, that they may very well be inadmissible unless you can get that witness to testify. If the witness is unavailable and you are called on to provide testimony regarding your interview of a witness, these additional details will help you immensely. If you are a busy LEO, you will not be able to testify adequately without recording these little details.

Given the importance of observations, and the rules of evidence regarding hearsay, know that your descriptions of what you see and hear are very important. Witness statements are good, but if you get those statements, make sure you get accurate contact and identifying information for those witnesses. If you cannot find them later to testify in trial, their statements may very well be out of reach.

Statements made by a defendant is one important exception to hearsay. You might hear such statements referred to as statements made against one's penal interest, confessions or admissions. If you have such evidence, make sure you properly document it.

Forms

Much of your professional writing will be written into or upon forms. Arrest reports, accident reports, evidence forms, contact cards, they will all have boxes requesting certain information. As a general matter, the purpose for such blocks is to guarantee that your report contains the most obvious data needed for the case. These blocks may require the name of the complainant, the address of the incident, a description of the suspect, etc. Some agencies have fairly detailed sections that require completion. Some are quite complex, and even confusing (see the section on **Organization**).

If you are providing certain information in these sections of the form, you should strongly consider omitting that information from your narrative. For example, if the suspect portion of the form already contains his height, weight, gender, hair and eye color, clothing, mannerisms, and demeanor, then those descriptors probably do not require further attention in your narrative. These sections all make up a single form. You should save the narrative portion for additional information not already contained elsewhere in your report. Use the narrative to tell the story and add unique information that was not already captured elsewhere. You could describe the suspect as follows:

The suspect, <u>as described above</u>, appeared very agitated and had a bleeding injury above his left eye.

Some officers simply do not complete the fill-in-the-blank portion of their reports, preferring to document everything in the narrative. That may be ok in some agencies, but understand that many agencies use the fill-in-the-blank portions for data collection, mandatory reporting, and analysis. This data collection can be very useful: analysts can review burglaries agency/county/state/nation wide and match suspects based on common data. If you leave these fields blank, your data will not be captured and your case may go unsolved because the report did not provide that data for analysis.

Beyond Reporting

Not all LEOs are first responders writing incident reports in their patrol cars. Many of you may need to draft affidavits, declarations and other documents, some of which will be eventually signed by a judge. This is an especially important subset of professional writing that you must master. Some of you will have the benefit of a prosecutor reviewing this writing and making the necessary corrections. Whether or not you have this benefit, your writing should be precise and free from errors.

You should apply all the rules we have discussed in this book. Avoid stilted and overly formal language. The one to watch out for in this context is referring to yourself as *Your Affiant*. Just say *I*. The judge knows you are the Affiant! It will significantly reduce space and make for a much more readable document.

Always describe your relevant experience and education in the beginning of your affidavit. This is a chance for you to introduce yourself to the court and to explain why the judge should believe you. Some jurisdictions have particular rules. Some jurisdictions require the affiant to be a state certified peace officer. If so, you must lay out that you meet the requirements to submit affidavits. Some LEOs call this their "hero sheet," and lay out all their particular training and experience. Whatever you call it, make it complete, complimentary, and relevant, and above all else, make sure you provide everything the judge will need to approve whatever you are asking for, whether it be an arrest warrant, search warrant or the like.

Remember, you will swear to the fact that everything contained therein is a true and accurate statement. Make sure you can honestly swear to that fact. This is not the time to be sloppy in your professional writing. There could be serious consequences for not taking sufficient time drafting this document. If you have someone helping you draft or edit your work, make doubly sure that you have read the final version very carefully before signing it and swearing to its veracity. Your reputation, and thus your career, depends on this.

A Word About E-writing

E-mails, text messages, PIN messages, SMS, even voice mails, anything digital that records something you are saying or writing, requires particular attention. These are communications that can stick around on someone's hard drive for years, unbeknownst to anyone. You must be careful with these mediums for communication. The most common mistake is speaking too casually, and without regard to the fact that these communications can actually be discoverable. E-mail exchanges between LEOs regarding cases are actually statements and will most likely have to be given to the defense when and if the case is charged and goes to trial.

Should you avoid abbreviations and lingo in these communications? Of course not; you only have so many characters you can type into a text message. These are not formal communications. You simply need to get a certain point across when sending a text. However, you should use caution with these mediums, as they are prone to be taken lightly; abbreviate as needed, just do not cross the line.

Furthermore, if an e-mail you send gets forwarded to someone else, eventually it could end up in the hands of someone you do not expect; from there it could find its way into a newspaper or defense attorney's inbox. For these reasons, you must make sure that you treat these communications as carefully as you do your affidavits, reports, and all the other mediums we discussed. Do not write in these mediums in a manner that suggests prejudice, uses foul or inappropriate language, or in any way could be used to discredit you or harm your reputation for speaking the truth.

These documents are generally not maintained as carefully as official documents, and could therefore be altered. Furthermore, they can survive far longer than some official records that are subject to destruction rules. In short: treat every communication as if they were going to be later read by a defense attorney, or your supervisor, or your spouse. If you would not tell these people in person what you are writing, then do not write it! I know more than one LEO that simply does not send text messages or e-mails. When you send one of these electronic messages to them, you get a telephone call in response. Think of it this way; if you are responsible for the arrest of a very wealthy person, that person will be willing to pay some private investigator a lot of money to dig up dirt on you. Do not let them have anything to find.

Final Thoughts

Once you have completed your professional writing, put it down. Walk away. Take some time if you have it. Return to it only after you have cleared your head. Then you should read it again, looking for mistakes, clarity, accuracy. Editing and proofreading is just as important as writing the report. The final product should be perfect.

I had an Evidence professor in law school who used to tell us that every year he sat in his office and read the Federal Rules of Evidence from cover to cover. He knew the rules by heart, but explained to us that every year he discovered some nuance, some language that he had not noticed before. It is like the preacher reading the Bible every day. Years and years later, that preacher may still find passages that suddenly seem relevant, or have some meaning not considered previously. This is one of the reasons why it is so important to read, re-read, then re-read again. This applies to your own reporting. If you write a report, review it immediately, then hand it in for processing, you are cheating yourself out of the ability to look at the document with fresh eyes. You will gloss over your own mistakes.

Additional Resources

There is a great website I have found called Wisc-Online. The website was created by faculty at the Wisconsin Technical College Program and it has some great ideas and resources. They actually have an interactive police report writing program that you can use. Try it at http://www.wisc-online.com. When you get there, click on the button marked "learning objects." Then look on the left for a drop down menu titled "General Education." Then click "Technical Reporting." You will then see the program, "Investigation Report Writing."

Here is another really fun website, sponsored by the publishing company Wadsworth. It is a template for a police report. The web link is very long, so do this: do a Google search for "Wadsworth" and "police report template." It will be your first hit. This website has an actual Microsoft Word version of a generic police report. There is no feedback on this one, but if you are new to law enforcement, you will find the exercise of completing a report worthwhile.

Even the website WikiHow has something to say about police report writing: http://www.wikihow.com/Write-a-Police-Report. Of course, Google is also in the mix and has collected dozens of police reports and related forms and templates here: http://website-tools.net/google-keyword/word/sample+police+report+template. This one is especially interesting, as it features forms and samples from all over the United States and overseas. Do a little research on your own and you will find an unlimited amount of resources on this topic.

I hope you have enjoyed this little book and learned something from it. If you are considering a career in law enforcement but have not yet embarked on your journey, pick up a copy of *How to Become a Police Officer: The Best Tactics to Get Police Officer Jobs and enter the Police Academy*, and you can get some good, straight forward advice on how to start that journey.

If you just want a little entertainment and maybe get some insight into the daily life of a uniformed beat cop, you will soon be able to check out my other book, *Police Daily Journal; Tongue in Cheek True Stories*. These are true stories about true events. I personally experienced each of them, and tried to select those that are indicative of what some of your first dispatches may be like. I also tried to use only those that provided some entertainment or comedic value. Like I have said before, you must find the humor in being a LEO. If you take yourself too seriously all the time, this job will weigh you down and cause emotional damage. Go to the end of my book and click the button to add your e-mail to my mailing list. I'll let you know when the book is released.

I wish you all the best of luck and am confident that if you paid attention to the content of this book, your writing will improve starting right now!

If you enjoyed reading this book, I hope you consider taking a look at some of my other books: *How to Become a Police Officer: The Best Tactics to Get Police Officer Jobs and enter the Police Academy*. And, coming in August 2020, *Grammar Saves Lives, Volume 2!*

Following is an excerpt from my book in progress, *Police Daily Journal; Tongue in Cheek True Stories:*

Excerpt from *Police Daily Journal; Tongue in Cheek True Stories*:

Day 8

Today I was assigned to our 344 beat, which meant I would spend almost my entire shift going from one silly call to another. 344 was a somewhat narrow but very long beat: I could spend the evening driving from one end of it to the other. What made it worse was that it was almost all strip malls and expensive neighborhoods with no highways. There would be nothing except for false residential alarms, accidents and silly disputes.

Furthermore, the officer assigned to 344 beat was partnered with the one assigned to 346 beat, and I knew that 346 would be empty for a while. The officer assigned to that beat had a reputation for sticking around the precinct for at least an hour after everyone else was in service. There was always a reason; "I had to discuss something with the Sergeant," or "I had to finish some paperwork before I left," or "I had to return a few calls from yesterday." Whatever the case, he was always the last officer in service. If you were his beat partner, you knew you would be handling things for yourself all evening.

As I will learn today, sometimes it doesn't always help to treat people with respect. Today, as I walked into the squad room, fifteen minutes early, my Sergeant was waiting for me. A dispute in progress was just announced over the radio in my beat, and the beat cop on the day shift was in court and could not respond. There was no-one to go except me and my friend Victor, who was in 348 that day; we had both arrived early to the precinct. We each grabbed a set of keys off the board and ran out the door. We were in service within five minutes and asked the dispatcher for the details. Apparently a pair of landlords were trying to kick out their tenants for failure to pay their rent on time. Alcohol was involved and the tenants were scared.

This was a problematic call for the police for several reasons. First and foremost, police officers cannot enforce contracts, or become involved in civil matters. If a tenant signs a lease with a landlord and then fails to pay the rent, the remedy is whatever is contemplated in the lease. Generally, the failure to pay rent leads to an eviction, which is a civil remedy. Police officers cannot enforce such a remedy. When dispatched to such a call, it usually infuriated the landlord to learn that we would be unable to assist them. This becomes even more problematic when alcohol is involved and when the dispute becomes immediate and physical. The dispatcher said we had all of the above.

It took us a while to find the house. It was all the way in the back of a very nice, very ritzy neighborhood. There were a lot of cul-de-sac streets and loops and traffic circles. Not an easy house to find. Once we did, we saw a Lexus in the driveway parked askew and the front door to the home was wide open. My partner and I cautiously approached and found a woman in the foyer in her fifties along with a much older woman, at least eighty years old, standing with a cane. At the top of a flight of stairs was a young foreign couple (turned out they were French) standing together, clearly frightened.

As we walked in we could clearly smell the unmistakable odor of an alcoholic beverage. It seemed to be coming from the women in the foyer. As we entered the room, the woman in her fifties turned to us and became quite animated. She was taller than me and quite portly.

"Good! The police are here. Go arrest them!"

With that, the woman grabbed me by the arm as if to launch me up the stairs. As a uniform police officer, it is quite offensive to be grabbed by someone. As she made her exclamation, it was clear that her breath was the source of the alcohol smell.

I tried to calm her down, but it was nearly impossible. I determined from her comments that she and her mother were at a bar when they decided to call their tenants and order them to be gone before they arrived back home. When they finally did leave the bar and found the tenants still there, the landlord/homeowners went ballistic. There had been no formal lease signed; the agreement was all oral. The tenants, who were in the United States on student visas, had not paid the rent because their sponsoring university abroad had been late depositing their stipend in their bank accounts.

I tried to explain that we could not enforce a lease or an eviction, and this succeeded only in making the woman more upset, louder, and more physical. She again grabbed my arm as if to send me vaulting upstairs. I pulled my arm away and warned her that the next time she touched me she was going to be arrested for battery. She didn't listen to me.

During this exchange, my partner, Victor, was standing by the woman's mother. The mother, it turned out, was also drunk, and was teetering on her little collapsible walking cane. She was silent, just watching the events unfold.

The younger woman made one more move toward my arm and grabbed it. I had had enough, and I yelled at her that she was under arrest. Apparently she did not want to be arrested. I had to wrestle her to the ground. Meanwhile, my partner was watching me with his mouth open, surprised perhaps that I was going to arrest her, or that she was resisting arrest, or maybe a little of both.

While he was watching in disbelief, the woman's 80-ish year old mother slid into action. She shuffled by my partner and up to the melee going on at her feet. I noticed her movement out of the corner of my eye, and turned to her just in time to see her with her arms over her head, clutching her collapsible cane, which she slammed down right between my eyes. That hurt! The cane collapsed, and as she reared up to hit me again, I did the only thing I could think of: I grabbed the younger woman in a one-armed bear hug, then grabbed the older woman by the shoulder. I pushed her backward toward my partner as hard as I could. She didn't weigh too much, and slammed into him and came to a landing at the foot of the stairs. I then finished wrestling the younger woman into handcuffs.

But it was far from over. We called for an ambulance for the older woman, but the younger one was still in the fight. She was trying to kick me, bite me, spit at me, whatever it took to get her revenge. Eventually I had to roll her onto her stomach and literally sit on her back. I was able, finally, to get the hand cuffs on her, but I had to remain sitting on her back like a bull rider. We waited for the ambulance to respond.

I thought that time would allow her head to clear somewhat, but I was wrong. The fire department arrived with the ambulance, and an old fire Lieutenant swaggered into the home. He had a long, old fashioned handlebar moustache, and had the general appearance of a cowboy from the Wild West. The Lieutenant asked to take a look at the woman I was sitting on, so without standing up, I crouched down and told her that the fire department was here and wanted to make sure she was not injured. I asked her if she was going to allow them to check on her welfare, and she nodded her assent. She was still panting and grunting, though. The Lieutenant approached, I stood up from her and helped her sit on the floor, and without pause, she somehow managed to lie back on her side and as hard as she could, kicked the Lieutenant in his private parts. He fell to the ground beside me, and I had to sit back down on the defendant. In the end, it took four of us to get her into the ambulance. At the jail, she was so brutal that she was strapped into something they called "The Chair." It was a chair that strapped the seated party at the head, chest, arms, legs and feet. She tried biting every deputy that came within two feet. I am honestly not sure what happened to the older woman; I only remember her complaining to the EMTs that I might have broken her hip.

After leaving them at the jail, I had to drive to the Magistrate's Office. I will explain this in more detail on another day, but generally speaking, when a police officer charged someone with a crime (with certain exceptions, like traffic code violations), that officer had a short window of time within which they had to go before a judge and prove that there was probable cause to support the arrest. That judge (in Georgia) was called a Magistrate. I intended to charge them both with battery, which, under Georgia law, meant any offensive touching. It was a misdemeanor, and included kicking someone, grabbing them, or biting them. Georgia also had a crime entitled aggravated assault that, in Georgia, essentially meant threatening to use or actually using a deadly weapon against another. This was a felony. In both cases, there were special provisions if they were committed upon a police officer or fireman.

I wasn't a big advocate of charging an old woman with aggravated assault on a peace officer (a police officer in Georgia is called, by statute, a peace officer), but when I explained what happened to the Magistrate, she informed me that the facts fit the offense and it was the most appropriate crime with which to charge her. That evening, I left her office with two felony warrants with multiple charges for their attack on me and the Fire Lieutenant. It was a little embarrassing, but only a little. What was even more embarrassing was the Polaroid my Sergeant took of my face when I returned to the precinct that night. I had a large goose egg right between my eyes and on my forehead from where I was struck with the cane. It was entered as evidence for my case.

I learned a lot from that encounter. I think the most obvious lesson was that even little old ladies can hurt you. If her walking cane was one inch to the left or right, I might have lost an eye. An officer can never, ever, let their guard down. With the right amount of alcohol and a little anger, even someone's grandmother could be pushed over the edge and might attack you.

I also learned that an officer may do themselves a disservice to try to downplay the criminal behavior of another. I had nothing to be embarrassed about by charging an 82 year old woman with a crime. What happened today was clearly a felony, and not a misdemeanor. I was physically attacked by someone with a weapon. That was a textbook case of aggravated assault. It was the responsibility of the Magistrate to determine whether there existed probable cause to support my allegation that a crime was committed, and it was clear from the facts that there was an aggravated assault. It would be up to the district attorney's office to determine the proper charges and punishment for that offense, and if that meant offering to let the old lady plea to a reduced offense and a light sentence, then so be it. We each had a role to play in the criminal justice system; mine was to report the facts and the prosecutor's was to prosecute. In this case, that is exactly what they did.

Other Books to Read

by Steven Starklight

How to Become a Police Officer: The Best Tactics to Get Police Officer Jobs and enter the Police Academy

Grammar Saves Lives, Volume 2 (Available in August 2020)

Golem

By Jonathan B. Zeitlin

Death and Repair; a Michael Hart Mystery

The Body in the Hole; The Undertaker Series, Book 1

The Body in the Bed; The Undertaker Series, Book 2

Made in the USA
Columbia, SC
23 December 2023